Editor
Eric Migliaccio

Managing Editor
Ina Massler Levin, M.A.

Illustrator
Jen Long

Cover Artist
Brenda Di Antonis

Art Coordinator
Kevin Barnes

Art Director
CJae Froshay

Imaging
Craig Gunnell

Publisher
Mary D. Smith, M.S. Ed.

ACTIVITIES for Oral Language Development

Performances
Drama
Speeches
Asking Questions
Telephone Etiquette

Author

Jennifer Overend Prior, Ph.D.
Jeanne Dustman, M.Ed.

Teacher Created Resources, Inc.
6421 Industry Way
Westminster, CA 92683
www.teachercreated.com

ISBN-1-4206-3393-7

©2005 Teacher Created Resources, Inc.

Made in U.S.A.

Table of Contents

Introduction

Activities for Oral Communication and Presentations Grades 3–5 offers a series of activities to introduce students to a wide variety of methods and uses of oral communication. In essence, this book is an invitation to play. Beginning at a very young age, children use play to explore different lifestyles. For instance, they may role play being a fireman or a bride—even "playing house" falls under this category of exploration. It is this attitude of play that allows children to develop new skills and explore new avenues that will become integral to their lives. In much the same way that the game of "dress up" allows children to try on new looks, this book provides children a chance to try on new ideas.

This book is divided into three major parts of oral communication:

1. Public Speaking

Students will explore various types of public speaking, such as:

- participating in group conversation
- reading aloud
- presenting reports
- interviewing
- talking on the telephone

2. Persuasive Speech

Students will learn the art of persuasion by participating in the following:

- developing and sharing opinions
- disagreeing in a nice way
- presenting reviews of books, movies, and events
- group discussion
- conflict resolution

3. Drama

Students will participate in the following:

- storytelling
- script memorization and performance
- puppet shows
- Reader's Theater
- presenting poetry

This book also provides planning pages to assist students in developing their oral presentations, as well as rubrics for evaluation and self-evaluation.

Use this book to enrich your classroom lessons. Use these ideas or add additional materials of your own to explore the art of oral communication.

Standards

The activities in this book are designed to meet McREL Standards. Used with permission of McREL (Copyright 2000 McREL, Mid-continent Research for Education and Learning. Telephone: 303-337-0990. Website: *www.mcrel.org*).

The following standards are for grades 3–5:

Standard 8, Grades 3-5, Benchmark 2:
❖ Asks questions in class when he or she is confused and to seek others' opinions and comments

Standard 8, Grades 3-5, Benchmark 4:
❖ Speaks clearly and at an audible level

Standard 8, Grades 3-5, Benchmark 7:
❖ Makes basic oral presentations to class (e.g., uses subject-related information and vocabulary; includes content appropriate to the audience; relates ideas and observations; incorporates visual aids or props; incorporates several sources of information)

Standard 8, Grades 3-5, Benchmark 8:
❖ Uses enunciation, eye contact, posture, gestures, and facial expressions appropriate for different situations

Standard 8, Grades 3-5, Benchmark 8:
❖ Uses pace, pitch, and vocabulary appropriate for different situations

Standard 8, Grades 3-5, Benchmark 9:
❖ Uses word choice appropriate for specific audiences and purposes

Standard 8, Grades 3-5, Benchmark 10:
❖ Organizes ideas for oral presentations (e.g., organizes ideas around major points)

You will also find activities that introduce students to the following more challenging McREL standards:

Standard 8, Grades 6-8, Benchmark 2:
❖ Responds to questions and comments by giving reasons in support of opinions and commenting on others' ideas

Standard 8, Grades 9-12, Benchmark 5:
❖ Makes formal presentations to the class (e.g., uses visual aids or technology to support presentation)

Standard 8, Grades 9-12, Benchmark 8:
❖ Responds to questions and feedback about own presentations

Delivery

Definition: Delivery is a combination of all the speaking skills used to convey ideas or communicate with the listeners.

Regularly review the following skills to improve students' deliveries:

○ Relax! Most people experience stage fright when they stand and speak in front of a group.

○ Breathe deeply and speak slowly to avoid a quivering or breathless voice.

○ Stand with one foot in front of the other and weight balanced to avoid that feeling of shaking and trembling. If your hands shake, hold them in front of you, rest them on the podium, or let them hang at your sides.

○ Concentrate on what you're saying, and the stage fright will pass.

○ Don't rush through your speech and speak too rapidly. Take your time and say each word distinctly.

○ Put notes on a large card or a page saver. This will help steady them if you tremble and will help you look calm. (An outline form is included on the next page.)

○ Don't read your speech from notes. Use an outline and talk to the listener. If the group is frightening, concentrate on one person at a time.

○ Vary the rate, pitch, volume, intensity, and rhythm of your voice. This is called vocal inflection.

○ Some movement for emphasis or to give you a relaxed look is good, but don't move back and forth or develop nervous mannerisms. Avoid wringing hands, tugging at clothing, or twisting hair.

○ Gestures are simply moving your hands to emphasize a point. It is good to talk with your hands, but plan small, relaxed gestures.

○ Grammar and vocabulary should be practiced ahead of time to avoid problems.

○ Avoid fill-in phrases, such as "you know," "uhh," "um," and "you see."

○ A mistake is a normal part of any learning experience. If you make one, correct it and go on.

○ Speaking is acting. Act like you are having a great time and your listeners will believe you.

Organization

The best method of organizing a speech is the three-point outline. It enables the speaker to tell at a glance exactly what point he or she is making. It is the roadmap for the speech. If you get confused, it steers you back on course.

Provide each student with a copy of the speech outline below for reference in future speech-writing activities.

I. Introduction and Attention Step

Use a joke or story as an attention step. It is also good to state your topic at the beginning.

II. Body (all basic content of the speech)

A. First Subpoint

1. Description

2. Provide details and supporting information.

B. Second Subpoint

1. Description

2. Provide details and supporting information.

C. Third Subpoint

1. Description

2. Provide details and supporting information.

III. Conclusion

Refer back to the attention step, and tie it all together.

6

Audience Etiquette and Participation

It is necessary to communicate to your students that the audience plays an important role during oral presentations. The audience can be polite and attentive and help the speaker to have an enjoyable experience, or they can be disrespectful and discourage the speaker.

Review the rules of audience etiquette below with your students. You may also want to post these rules for future reference.

Audience Etiquette

○ Pay attention when a student is speaking.

○ Give the speaker appropriate eye contact.

○ Listen attentively.

○ Stay quiet unless invited to do otherwise by the speaker.

○ Stay seated.

○ Do not make comments during the presentation unless asked by the speaker.

○ Do not make fun of the speaker in any way.

○ Applaud (sincerely) after the presentation.

○ If asked to complete an evaluation of the speaker, be kind and offer both compliments and helpful suggestions.

Explain to the students that some of the oral communication activities they will participate in will be casual, but many will be much more formal. For some of these presentations they will be asked to evaluate their classmates, and they will also be evaluated themselves.

Express to the students that these evaluations are designed to assist with improving oral communication. Encourage them to remember the following as they complete these evaluations of their classmates:

1. The speaker might be nervous. Pay attention and keep a pleasant look on your face.

2. Think about the good things you notice. Be sure to write nice things about the speech.
   - Is the speech interesting?
   - Does the speaker make eye contact?
   - Can you hear the speaker clearly?

3. When you notice areas for improvement, express them positively. Offer suggestions for changing, not just criticism.

4. After the presentation is finished, say something nice (out loud) to the speaker. Congratulate him or her on a job well done.

5. Remember that the next speaker could be you! Treat your classmates as you would like them to treat you.

Ideas for Public Performances

You'll find that your students are more inspired to speak publicly when they have a reason to do so. This involves more than just making presentations for their classmates. The following are ideas for giving your students the opportunity to perform in public:

❖ Morning Announcements

Most schools have daily morning announcements communicated by loudspeaker or live recordings. Ask your principal for permission to periodically take a few minutes of the announcements for your students to perform poetry readings, Reader's Theater radio shows, book or movie reviews, or persuasive speeches.

❖ Video Recordings

Each time your students present oral reports, plays, poetry readings, and other performances, videotape their productions. At the end of the school year, invite parents to send in VCR tapes and duplicate the productions onto tapes for the students to take home. They will then have a documented record of their performances throughout the year.

❖ Class Performances

Arrange to have your students present to younger students or other classes in your grade level. Productions for other classes will likely motivate your students to do their very best.

❖ Parent Events

Your school probably has numerous events throughout the year where parents participate in school activities, such as Back-to-School Night, Open House, etc. Be sure to include oral communication presentations as a part of the festivities.

❖ Lunchroom Performances

A few times a year, arrange to have your students present book/movie reviews, Reader's Theaters, poetry readings, etc., in the cafeteria during lunchtime. You'll need to make arrangements for a sound system so your students will be heard above the lunchroom "roar."

❖ School Assemblies

Arrange to have time during assemblies throughout the year in which your students can perform their most recent productions.

❖ Book Talks

Ask your coworkers to allow your students to present book talks to their students. Your students can perform these during those last few minutes of the end of the school day. It gives your students the opportunity to write book reviews for a clear purpose and might inspire other students to do a bit more reading.

❖ Coffeehouse Performances

Schedule a special coffeehouse day/evening for students or parents. Set up your classroom in a coffeehouse setting with tables, tablecloths, dimmed lights, candles, light music, etc. Serve drinks and light snacks for the guests. Then have each of your students prepare a short oral presentation of poetry, a short play, or Reader's Theater to perform for the guests.

Getting Started with Public Speaking

To initiate public speaking with your students, begin informally by having them get to know one another. The following activities provide creative ways for students to introduce themselves to their classmates.

Introduce Yourself

Objective: Ease students into speaking in front of a group with the following activity.

1. Gather your students together for introductions.
2. Tell the students that each of them will introduce him- or herself by sharing the following information:
   - name
   - age
   - something about his or her family
   - favorite thing about school
3. Allow students a few minutes to think about what they will share.
4. Allow each student to share this information with the group.
5. After each student shares, encourage classmates to ask a few questions to clarify information.

Extension: As students become more comfortable with one another, have them participate in a more formal introduction.
  1. Distribute copies of the "Introduce Yourself" sheet on page 16.
  2. Have each student complete the page and then practice giving their introduction in front of a partner.
  3. Finally, have students stand before the class to introduce themselves.

Take a Square

Objective: This fun activity allows students to share more information with their classmates.

Materials: roll of bathroom tissue

1. Pass a roll of bathroom tissue around to the students.
2. Instruct the students to take at least two but not more than 10 squares of tissue.
3. After all students have taken the desired number of tissue squares, explain that the number of squares taken equals the number of facts students need to share about themselves. For example, if a student took two squares, he or she must share two pieces of personal information. If the student took 10 squares, he or she must share 10 things.
4. Have students take turns sharing information about themselves.
5. Encourage classmates to ask questions to clarify the information shared.

Getting Started *(cont.)*

Select Words Carefully

Objective: This activity helps students eliminate unnecessary words when speaking.

Materials: student copies of "Story Evaluation" (page 17)

1. Explain to the students that often when people speak, they use words that are not needed. Provide an example of this by reading the following two stories.

Story #1

The other day, I, um, went to the park, um, with my friend Gina. We, like, wanted to ride our bikes on the paths, you know, but the wind was, like, blowing so hard. Um, we could hardly, um, ride our bikes because, like, the wind almost blew us over, you know. Finally, we just, like, went home because, like, we weren't having very much fun.

Story #2

The other day, I went to the park with my friend Gina. We wanted to ride our bikes on the paths, but the wind was blowing so hard. We could hardly ride our bikes because the wind almost blew us over! Finally, we just went home because we weren't having very much fun.

---

2. Ask the students to compare the two stories and offer their comments about them.
3. Explain that there are words we use in casual conversation that should not be used in public speaking. Sometimes we use the words so often that it is difficult to speak without them.
4. Ask each student to think of a short story to share. Then divide the students into groups of three or four.
5. Provide each group member with a copy of the "Story Evaluation" sheet on page 17.
6. Ask students to take turns sharing their stories in the group. Group members should listen for the use of unnecessary words and record them on the sheet.
7. Have group members discuss their use of unnecessary words and encourage them to practice retelling their stories without them.

Getting Started *(cont.)*

Speak Up!

Objective: Help students speak in a way that can be clearly understood.

Materials: "Public Speaking Evaluation Sheet" (optional, page 19)

1. Gather students together and read the following text in a ***very quiet*** voice:

   "Today we're going to work on speaking clearly. If you speak too quietly, it is difficult for people to hear you. So, we are going to practice speaking up and speaking clearly."

2. After you finish reading the text, ask the students if they are ready to get started. Ask them what they are going to practice in the activity.

3. The students will likely say they were not able to hear or understand you.

4. Tell them that this is a problem with many people when speaking in public: they either don't speak loudly enough or they don't enunciate their words. Explain that *enunciate* means to pronounce words clearly.

5. Read the text from step 1 again, this time using an appropriate volume. Draw students' attention to the difference between the two times you read it.

6. Have students gather in small groups to tell short stories about recent events. Have them focus on speaking with appropriate volume (not too loud, not too soft). Have them concentrate on enunciating their words, as well.

7. You may want to have students use the evaluation sheet (page 19) to record their group members' progress.

Got My Eye on You!

Objective: When speaking in public, some people avoid making eye contact. Help students give appropriate eye contact with this activity.

Materials: one copy of "Public-Speaking Tips" (page 18)

1. Begin the activity by standing in front of the students. Explain to them that they will be learning about where to look and how to stand when speaking in front of others.

2. While you are explaining this to the students, do the following:

   ➤ look at the floor
   ➤ look up at the ceiling
   ➤ shuffle your feet
   ➤ wring your hands together
   ➤ put your hands in and out of your pockets
   ➤ tap your legs
   ➤ take deep breathes and sigh

3. Ask the students to tell what they noticed about your behaviors.

4. Draw their attention to the fact that these behaviors convey nervousness and should be avoided when speaking in public. Explain that when speaking to a group, the speaker's eyes should scan back and forth across the group, looking at the people. It is also appropriate to look just above the listeners' heads.

5. Post a list of proper behaviors (see page 18).

6. Divide the students into groups of six; have students take turns telling about a favorite book they read. Have students focus on making eye contact and standing still while speaking.

7. Students can use the public-speaking evaluation sheet to record their group members' progress.

Presenting a Report

Report presentations are a natural way to add public-speaking experiences to your classroom routine. These activities provide ideas for presenting book reports and research reports.

Planning an Oral Book Report

Objective: Book reports don't always have to be written. Giving an oral report is an important skill for students to learn.

Materials: student copies of "Planning an Oral Book Report" sheet (page 20)

1. Explain that when presenting an oral report, a person should tell the title of the book, the author, the main characters, and important story events.
2. The person can also tell about his or her favorite part and whether or not he or she recommends that others read the book.
3. This can seem like a daunting task, so provide each student with a copy of the planning sheet on page 20.
4. Encourage students to practice presenting their oral reports before presenting to the class.

Character Report

Objective: Allow your students to add creative flair to oral book reports by acting as characters in stories they have read.

Materials: student copies of "Character Report" (page 21)

1. Ask the students to think about a book they have recently read. Then tell them that they will each pretend to be a character in the story.
2. Distribute copies of "Character Report" (page 21).
3. Have each student answer the questions as if he or she is that character.
4. Then have each student plan a costume to wear that represents the chosen character.
5. Finally, have each student present the oral book report from the character's point of view.

Research Report

Objective: After writing research reports, give your students the opportunity to present them orally to the class.

Materials: student copies of "Report Planning Sheet" (page 22)

1. Gather students together and explain that they will be presenting their research reports to the class using an oral presentation.
2. Ask the students to think about the content of their reports and which parts would be the most important to share.
3. Explain that when presenting a report, the speaker should not read it directly from the paper. This kind of presentation should be more casual, with the speaker presenting just the most important points.
4. Also, tell the students that an oral report presentation should last only about three to five minutes.
5. Distribute copies of "Report Planning Sheet" on page 22.
6. After students complete the page, have each student practice the presentation aloud.

Presenting a Report *(cont.)*

Using Note Cards

Objective: Assist your students with their oral report presentations by teaching them to use note cards.

Materials: student copies of "Note Cards" (page 23)

1. Explain that when giving a presentation, it can be useful to have note cards of reminders for what will be said.

2. Tell students that a note card should only have a few words on it to remind you of what to say. For example, a note card for a presentation about whales might look like this:

Whales
Kinds of whales
Size
Food
Locations
In danger
Where to see

3. Duplicate and cut apart the note cards on page 23. Distribute one note card to each student.

4. Assist the students with selecting words that best represent the information they want to share.

5. Explain that when presenting their reports, they can hold the note card and glance at it occasionally for reminders.

Multimedia Presentations

Objective: Help your students add pizzazz to their oral presentations by adding multimedia displays.

Materials: "Multimedia Presentations" (page 24)

1. Gather students together and tell them that many presenters use visual aids to assist them with presenting information to their audiences.

2. Ask the students to brainstorm the kinds of visual aids that could be used, such as the following:

   ➢ posters   ➢ PowerPoint presentations

   ➢ models   ➢ overhead transparencies

3. Explain that posters and models often show diagrams or graphs related to the topic. PowerPoint presentations and overhead transparencies serve as "note cards" that remind the presenter of information to be shared. They also help the audience to follow along with the information presented.

4. Instruct students to think of the best visual aid to use for their presentations. Display a copy of page 24 to assist students with ideas for their multimedia presentations.

Questioning Strategies

Public speaking often involves asking questions of others. Assist your students with questioning strategies using the following activities:

Open-ended Questions

Objective: Assist your students in asking questions that provide detailed information.

Materials: "Complex Questions" (page 25)

1. Explain to the students that some questions require complex answers and some only require simple answers. Here are some examples of each type of question:

Simple	Complex
➢ How are you?	➢ Why do you like playing soccer?
➢ Do you like that?	➢ What does the color red remind you of?
➢ What is your favorite color?	➢ What do you like about the taste of pizza?

2. Draw students' attention to the way the questions are asked and the kinds of answers they require. Explain that questions requiring detailed answers are called open-ended. This means that the answers are more involved than "yes" or "no" or other one-word replies.

3. Provide students with a copy of "Complex Questions" (page 25) to practice creating questions that require detailed answers.

4. When students have completed their pages, have them meet with other students to compare their newly created open-ended questions.

What the Future Holds

Objective: Use this activity to help your students generate questions.

1. Ask your students to think about their plans for the future, such as:
    - ➢ places they would like to visit
    - ➢ plans for higher education (college, etc.)
    - ➢ career choices
    - ➢ skills or hobbies they would like to learn

2. Divide the students into pairs.

3. Have the students meet with their partners to tell each other (only briefly) about their future plans.

4. Then have each student make a list of questions to ask his or her partner about these plans. Here are a few examples:
    - ➢ How long have you wanted to do this?
    - ➢ Why is this interesting to you?
    - ➢ What steps will you take to do this?

5. Remind students to ask open-ended questions that require more than just "yes" or "no" answers.

6. Have the partners meet together again to ask and record their questions.

7. Finally, have the students introduce their partners to the class, telling about their future plans.

Questioning Strategies *(cont.)*

Creating Interview Questions

Objective: This activity helps your students to ask and answer questions from a story.

Materials: student copies of "Interview Questions" (page 26), chalkboard and chalk

1. Explain to the students that we often need to find out information by asking a person a series of questions. Ask them to think about people who could answer questions for them about the following:

   - ➢ school events
   - ➢ sports
   - ➢ music

   - ➢ going to college
   - ➢ good study habits
   - ➢ working for a television station

2. Select a particular topic and ask the students to think of someone who might be an expert in this area. For example, a student who gets good grades might be an expert on good study habits.

3. Next, ask the students to think of open-ended questions that could be asked of the expert. List the questions on the chalkboard. Here are some examples of questions to ask an expert on getting good grades:

   - ➢ Why do you think you are a good student?
   - ➢ How much time do you spend doing homework?
   - ➢ What do you do to prepare for a test?
   - ➢ Are there ever times when you study with someone else? When?
   - ➢ What is your best tip for getting good grades in school?

4. Draw students' attention to the fact that these are all open-ended questions that require more complex answers.

5. Distribute copies of "Interview Questions" on page 26.

6. Instruct each student to select a person who would be an expert about a certain topic and then write open-ended questions that could be asked of this person. (Encourage each student to choose a person that he or she could actually interview.)

7. Instruct each student to check each question to make sure it cannot be answered by just a "yes" or "no" answer.

Introduce Yourself

Directions: Answer the following questions about yourself. Practice a self-introduction using this information. Try to memorize your introduction.

1. Where were you born? _____

2. How many people are in your family? _____

3. Do you have pets? _____

4. What is your favorite food? _____

5. What is your least favorite food? _____

6. What is your favorite sport? _____

7. What do you like to do in your free time? _____

   _____

8. What is your favorite smell? _____

9. What sound do you hate? _____

10. What is one thing you would like to change in the world? _____

   _____

Story Evaluation.

Directions: Complete an evaluation as a classmate tells a story. Fill in a checkmark each time you hear the student use an unnecessary word. Then write a comment or suggestion to assist the student with improving his or her storytelling.

Speaker: _____

Unnecessary Words

➤ Like ☑ ☑ ☑ ☑ ☑ ☑ ☑ ☑ ☑ ☑

➤ You know ☑ ☑ ☑ ☑ ☑ ☑ ☑ ☑ ☑ ☑

➤ Um ☑ ☑ ☑ ☑ ☑ ☑ ☑ ☑ ☑ ☑

➤ Uh ☑ ☑ ☑ ☑ ☑ ☑ ☑ ☑ ☑ ☑

Comments: _____

_____

Directions: Complete an evaluation as a classmate tells a story. Fill in a checkmark each time you hear the student use an unnecessary word. Then write a comment or suggestion to assist the student with improving his or her storytelling.

Speaker: _____

Unnecessary Words

➤ Like ☑ ☑ ☑ ☑ ☑ ☑ ☑ ☑ ☑ ☑

➤ You know ☑ ☑ ☑ ☑ ☑ ☑ ☑ ☑ ☑ ☑

➤ Um ☑ ☑ ☑ ☑ ☑ ☑ ☑ ☑ ☑ ☑

➤ Uh ☑ ☑ ☑ ☑ ☑ ☑ ☑ ☑ ☑ ☑

Comments: _____

_____

Public–Speaking Tips

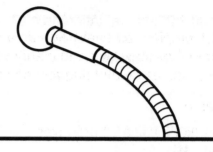

○ Look back and forth at people in the group or look just above their heads.

○ Speak loud enough for everyone to hear, but not too loud.

○ Stand with hands to your side or hold a note card.

○ Keep your feet still.

○ Don't rock back and forth.

○ Avoid using the words "like," "um," "uh," and "you know."

Evaluation Sheet

Directions: Complete an evaluation as a classmate speaks. Circle your response. Write a comment or suggestion to clarify your response. Be sure to write positive comments, as well as helpful suggestions for improvement.

Speaker's name:

1. The speaker's voice volume was **appropriate** **too soft** **too loud**

Explain: _____

2. The speaker **gave eye contact** **avoided eye contact**

Explain: _____

3. The speaker **stood still** **rocked back and forth** **looked nervous**

Explain: _____

4. The speaker **used unnecessary words** **used appropriate words**

Explain: _____

5. The speaker **read the words** **spoke naturally**

Explain: _____

Directions: Complete an evaluation as a classmate speaks. Circle your response. Write a comment or suggestion to clarify your response. Be sure to write positive comments, as well as helpful suggestions for improvement.

Speaker's name:

1. The speaker's voice volume was **appropriate** **too soft** **too loud**

Explain: _____

2. The speaker **gave eye contact** **avoided eye contact**

Explain: _____

3. The speaker **stood still** **rocked back and forth** **looked nervous**

Explain: _____

4. The speaker **used unnecessary words** **used appropriate words**

Explain: _____

5. The speaker **read the words** **spoke naturally**

Explain: _____

Planning an Oral Book Report

Directions: Use this page to help you plan an oral report about a book you have read. Read through this page to remember what you wrote. Practice saying your report out loud before presenting it to the class.

The name of the book I read was _____

The author of the book is _____

The book was about a main character named _____

This character _____

_____

_____

In the story, these things happened: _____

_____

_____

My favorite part of the story was _____

_____

_____

I (circle one)   **do   do not**   recommend this book because _____

_____

_____

Character Report

Directions: Think of a book you recently read. Select a character from the story. Answer the questions below as if you are that character.

Book title: _____

Author: _____

Character's name: _____

Who are you? _____

What is your age? _____

Who else is in the story? _____

_____

_____

What happens to you in the story? _____

_____

_____

_____

_____

How do you feel about this? _____

_____

_____

_____

What kind of costume could you wear when presenting your character report? _____

_____

_____

_____

Practice your report, pretending that you are the character.

Report Planning Sheet

Directions: Answer the questions below to assist you with your oral research report.

1. What is your topic?_____

2. What were three important questions that were answered through your research? What information did you find to answer these questions?

   Question #1: _____

   Answer: _____

   _____

   _____

   Question #2: _____

   Answer: _____

   _____

   _____

   Question #3: _____

   Answer: _____

   _____

   _____

3. Is there information you would still like to know about this topic? If so, what is it?

   _____

   _____

4. What do you think is the most important information your audience should know about your topic?

   _____

Note Cards

Directions: Use one note card to write reminders to help you with your presentation. Write only one or two words on each line. These words will help to remind you of the information you want to share with your audience.

Topic: _____

Important information: _____

_____

_____

Unanswered questions: _____

_____

_____

Final thoughts: _____

_____

_____

Directions: Use one note card to write reminders to help you with your presentation. Write only one or two words on each line. These words will help to remind you of the information you want to share with your audience.

Topic: _____

Important information: _____

_____

_____

Unanswered questions: _____

_____

_____

Final thoughts: _____

_____

_____

Multimedia Presentations

Directions: Add pizzazz to your oral presentations by adding multimedia displays. Here are some ideas you can use:

Media	Presentation
Poster	On a sheet of poster board or tag board, make a poster with a drawing of the subject of your presentation. Use markers, tempera paint, glitter paint, or other decorative items to add words and pictures to the poster.
Diagram	Create a diagram of the subject of your presentation. Make your diagram on a sheet of construction paper or on a large sheet of poster board. Be sure to use bold colors in the diagram and to label the parts clearly.
Graph	Create a graph showing information you gathered in your research. Be sure to clearly label the parts of the graph. Use bold colors.
Model	Make a model of the subject of your presentation. Think about using salt dough*, clay, or papier mâché for your model.
Overhead Transparency	Make overhead transparencies showing important facts about your topic. Use a wipe-off marker to write the facts on a transparency sheet.
PowerPoint Presentation	Have an adult assist you with creating a presentation using Microsoft PowerPoint. Try to use text and graphics on your slides.
Artifact	Create an artifact of an item that represents your topic.
Video Clip	Select a video clip related to your topic to show to your audience. Be sure the clip is short—a minute, at most.
Photo	Locate a photo related to your topic to display during your presentation.
Props	Display props related to your topic.
Experiment	Conduct a demonstration or experiment related to your topic.
Handout	Create a handout to give to audience members featuring important information related to the topic.

*Note: To make a batch of salt dough, mix one cup of salt, two cups of flour, and one cup of water. If desired, add food coloring to the dough or paint the salt dough model after it dries.

Complex Questions

Directions: Answer each simple question with a one-word answer. Then change each question below into an open-ended question. Rewrite it on the line. Compare your open-ended questions with classmate's.

1. How are you today? _____

   _____

2. What is your favorite animal? _____

   _____

3. How is the weather outside? _____

   _____

4. Do you like music? _____

   _____

5. Do you have a hobby? _____

   _____

6. Do you like movies? _____

   _____

7. Who is your best friend? _____

   _____

8. If you could visit anywhere in the world, where would you go? _____

   _____

9. What is your favorite subject in school? _____

   _____

10. Where were you born? _____

   _____

Interview Questions

Directions: Create open-ended questions to ask someone you know.

Name of Interviewee: _____

General questions about the person's area of expertise:

1. _____
2. _____
3. _____

Questions about how the person feels about this subject:

1. _____
2. _____
3. _____

Helpful information this person could offer you:

1. _____
2. _____
3. _____

Additional questions:

1. _____
2. _____
3. _____

Asking Questions

Simple questions elicit knowledge-level answers such as "yes," "no," or a word or two. Most questions are like this. Higher-level questions require more complex answers and involve higher-level thinking.

Questions involving these three skills typically elicit lower-level answers:

- ❖ Knowledge ❖ Comprehension ❖ Application

Questions involving these three skills typically elicit higher-level answers:

- ❖ Analysis ❖ Synthesis ❖ Evaluation

The objective of these lessons is to teach students to ask questions that will provide optimal information. Through these lessons, students should learn to align the questions that they ask with the information that they want to obtain.

Let the Question Fit the Answer

1. Explain to the class that the way a question is asked usually determines the quality of the answer.
2. Give examples of questions that require one-word answers and questions that require an explanation.

Questions that Require One-Word Answers	Questions that Require Explanation
➤ Did you have a good day?	➤ What did you do today?
➤ Was that a good book?	➤ What was the book about?

3. Ask students to think of examples and write them on the chalkboard.
4. Ask students which kind of answer they prefer to give when questioned and which kind of answer they prefer to receive when they ask a question.
5. Give several examples of conversational questions and ask student volunteers to answer with a simple answer and also with a complex one.

   Example question: What kind of day did you have?
   Simple answer: A good day.
   Complex answer: It was really a great day. I wore my new jeans and felt great. I saw Paul before school, and he talked to me! He even sat with me at lunch and then walked me home from school. It was such a great day!

6. Instruct students to be aware of questions that they are asked during the next few days. Direct them to record the questions and answers in a journal. Have them mark whether the questions required simple or complex answers.

Asking Questions *(cont.)*

Alike or Different

Objective: Classrooms consist of many different kinds of people, yet in spite of their differences, there are many similarities. This is true of any group, organization, community, and even the world. One way to find out how similar or different people are is through questioning.

Materials: chart paper and marker, student copies of "Personal Questions" (optional, page 36)

1. Talk briefly about the process of learning about others.
2. Explain that one way we learn about others is by asking questions.
3. Review questioning techniques that elicit limited information and those that elicit complex information.
4. Choose two volunteers who are willing to answer questions about themselves.
5. Instruct the class to ask questions of the two volunteers. Remind them to structure their questions according to the kind of information that they want to learn.
6. Record the answers to their questions on a chart with two columns, one labeled "Simple" and one "Complex."
7. Close the lesson by discussing what was learned about the volunteers and how alike or different they are.
8. Discuss the questions that were the easiest to ask and answer.

> **Extension:** Scaffold this activity by having the class create categories from which to ask questions. Have students create a personal list of questions using page 36 to assist them with question asking.

Who Did It?

Objective: Questioning is an important part of solving problems. This activity provides practice in questioning by engaging students in a mystery.

Materials: student copies of "Solve the Mystery" (page 37)

1. Read a mystery story to the class, such as "The Island of the Skog" by Steven Kellogg.
2. Stop reading before the mystery is solved.
3. Distribute student copies of page 37. Instruct students to write down the questions that they think of as they ponder the solution to the mystery.
4. Ask students to read their questions aloud to the class. Encourage them to listen to classmates' questions, which might inspire more of their own questioning.
5. Read the remainder of the story and direct students to answer their questions based on the information in the story.

Asking Questions (cont.)

Observe and Question

Objective: Sometimes we process information through questioning. This activity provides practice in synthesizing information through questioning.

General Materials: chalkboard and chalk, see Experiments #1 and #2 for additional materials

1. Conduct two related science experiments. Be sure to allow the students to first use the materials to try to light a light bulb on their own. If they have trouble figuring it out, have them use the directions below.

Experiment #1

Materials: C or D battery, stainless steel table fork and spoon, a flashlight bulb, tape

Directions:

➢ Turn the battery upside-down so that the positive end faces down.

➢ Tape a flashlight bulb across the flat (negative) end of the battery.

➢ Touch the tines of a stainless steel dinner fork to the metal end of the flashlight bulb.

➢ Touch the rounded part of a stainless steel teaspoon to the positive end of the battery.

➢ Touch the handles of the spoon and the fork together. The bulb should light.

Experiment #2

Materials: lemon, brass thumbtack, steel paperclip, two pieces of copper wire, a flashlight bulb

Directions:

➢ Unwind a paper clip and stick one end in one side of the lemon and the thumbtack in the opposite side of the lemon.

➢ Trim one inch of the plastic covering from each end of the two pieces of wire. The bare ends should reveal two thin wires. Twist these wires together at each end.

➢ Attach one piece of wire to the paperclip and the other wire to the thumbtack.

➢ Touch the two free wire ends to the two bumps on the bottom of the flashlight bulb. The bulb should light.

2. Discuss the variables and outcomes of each experiment.

3. Explain that questioning classmates in a casual conversational manner is a great way to make sense of new concepts. Instruct students to think of questions that help explain and connect the two experiments.

4. Record the questions on the chalkboard for all to see.

5. Compare the processes and results. Elicit questions as to what happened and why the lights were lighted.

Extension: Show students two bugs (or pictures of two bugs). Direct them to ask questions about the two bugs. Write their questions on the chalkboard. Instruct students to locate information about the bugs and answer their questions.

Responding to Questions

It is important for students to know what response is appropriate to a given situation or audience. The purpose of this section is to provide practice with giving responses.

Code Switching

Objective: This activity provides practice in responding differently to different audiences within the same situation.

Materials: "Scenario Cards" (page 38)

1. Duplicate and cut apart the scenario cards on page 38.
2. On each card, write the names of two or three students who will be required to respond.
3. Instruct a volunteer to select one card and read the scenario. The students whose names are on the card will respond to it.
4. Instruct the volunteer to respond in the appropriate way to each of the students as they answer. (In the example below, the volunteer would play the role of the parents and the friend.)

You got a perfect score on your math test. Your friend's dad congratulates you.

- ✳ What will you say to your friend's dad?
- ✳ What will you say to your friend?

At an art gallery, you see a painting that you really don't like.

- ✳ What would you say about it to your friend?
- ✳ What would you say about it to the artist?

---

5. Ask the class to listen and either agree with the students' responses or offer alternatives.
6. Instruct the students to create some of their own scenarios to use in future lessons.

Attention to Detail

Objective: There are times when it is important to remember details so that they can be included in a response. This activity is designed to provide practice in observing and reporting details.

1. Show a detailed photograph or painting to a group of students.
2. Instruct them to describe the picture to the rest of the class, including as much detail as possible.
3. Show three pictures to the entire class, including the picture that was described.
4. Instruct the class to choose the picture that was described to them by the group of students.
5. Ask what details helped them to identify the original picture.

Extension: Show the class a picture and ask for volunteers to share their responses to the picture.

Responding to Questions *(cont.)*

Open or Closed

Objective: A response can be open, inviting to further conversation; or it can be closed, ending the conversation. Students should be aware of their responses and the effect they have on others.

1. Brainstorm responses that invite more conversation and list them on the chalkboard. (See below for a few examples.)

2. Brainstorm responses that close conversations and list them on the board. (See below for a few examples.)

   Example Question: How do you feel on a Saturday morning?

Open (Invites more conversation)	Closed (Ends conversation)
I feel excited to go outside to play.	Good.

   Question: What is your favorite thing to do when you have a whole day to yourself?

Open (Invites more conversation)	Closed (Ends conversation)
I like to play video games and see my friend.	Nothing.

   Question: If you could have a pet, what animal would you choose and why?

Open (Invites more conversation)	Closed (Ends conversation)
I love cats. They are so mysterious.	Cats.

3. Ask for volunteers to role-play scenarios using both kinds of responses.

4. Discuss how each kind of response made the students feel.

5. Instruct students to be aware of responses that they make or that are made to them in conversations during the week.

6. Instruct them to keep a log of responses that made them feel good about their conversations.

Emotional Response Charade

Objective: Responses can be shaped by emotions. A response can show how a person feels or what he or she might be going through. It is important for students to identify responses and their causes.

Materials: "Sentence Cards" (page 39), "Spinner Pattern" (page 40), brass fastener, paperclip

1. Duplicate and cut apart the sentence cards on page 39.

2. Duplicate the spinner wheel on page 40. Insert brass fastener through the center dot. Then attach a paperclip to the fastener to serve as a spinner.

3. Select a student to take a sentence card, and then spin the spinner (so classmates don't see).

4. The student then reads the sentence using the emotion indicated on the spinner.

5. Ask classmates to identify the emotion by listening to the response.

Extensions: Instruct students to use only nonverbal or one-word responses.

Responding to Questions *(cont.)*

Response Relay

Objective: This activity uses the standard relay format to provide practice with response.

1. Instruct the class to create a list of situations that warrant responses.
2. Write the situations on index cards.
3. Divide the class into two teams.
4. Select one card and read the situation written on the card.
5. Direct one person from each team to react to the situation.
6. Award one point to the team whose representative reacts first. The reaction must be appropriate in order for the point to be awarded.

Response Charades

Objective: This activity invites creative nonverbal responses to verbal prompts.
Materials: "Charade Cards" (page 41)

1. Duplicate and cut apart the charade cards on page 41.
2. Select three volunteers. Give each one card to read.
3. Have one student pantomime the situation written on the card, while the other two students watch and respond nonverbally to what is happening.
4. Instruct the class to determine the situation being pantomimed and talk about the various nonverbal responses.
5. Discuss the importance of response and what can be learned from observing responses.

Who Said That?

Objective: Many times different people will respond to the same situation differently. In this activity, students role-play responses that various people might have to a given situation.
Materials: index cards

1. Write questions on index cards and put them in a stack. Here are a few examples:

What is your favorite movie?	Do you want to go to the museum on Saturday?	What kind of music do you like?

2. Ask students to think of people that they encounter in their lives. Examples might include a teacher, a parent, a young child, a grandfather, etc.
3. List the people that students think of on the chalkboard.
4. Ask for a volunteer to select a question card and respond to the question in the way one of the people would probably respond.
5. Instruct the class to guess which person was being imitated.
6. Discuss why responses vary and how responses sometimes change over time.

Extension: Instruct students to add actions and body language to their responses.

Telephone Etiquette

Telephones provide a link to the outside world as students talk with family members and friends. It is important that children learn appropriate etiquette for telephone conversations.

What Is Appropriate?

Objective: It is important to find out what students already know about appropriate telephone etiquette. This activity is designed to activate students' prior knowledge in order to determine appropriate telephone etiquette.

Materials: "Telephone Conversation Scenarios" (page 42), "Telephone Etiquette Journal" (page 43)

1. Ask students to think of situations in which it is necessary or helpful to talk on the telephone.
2. List those situations on the chalkboard.
3. Ask students to share their ideas about telephone manners.
4. List their ideas on the chalkboard.
5. Choose two volunteers to role-play a telephone conversation using disconnected telephones as props.
6. Duplicate and cut apart the telephone conversation scenarios (page 42).
7. Ask two volunteers to select a card and role-play the telephone conversation. They should use good telephone manners.
8. Then select two more volunteers to role-play the same scenario, this time using bad manners.
9. Ask the students how they feel when someone has bad telephone manners.
10. Direct them to keep track of their telephone conversations during the next week and note examples of good and bad telephone manners in a telephone etiquette journal (page 43).

Taking Messages

Objective: It is important for students to learn to take accurate and appropriate telephone messages. Misunderstandings can easily arise from a message that is confusing.

Materials: sheets of acetate (one for each small group), wipe-off markers, overhead projector

1. Begin by telling the class of a time when you received a confusing message and were inconvenienced or embarrassed as a result.
2. Invite students to share experiences that they have had where a message conveyed incorrect information.
3. Brainstorm what information a good message should include.
4. Tell students that they will each work with a partner to design a message format that will help a person take an accurate and complete message.
5. Distribute sheets of acetate and wipe-off markers on which students create message formats.
6. Ask for volunteers to share their message formats using an overhead projector.

Telephone Etiquette *(cont.)*

Telephone Responses

Objective: This activity is designed to provide practice for responding when talking on the telephone.

Materials: "Telephone Etiquette Journal" (page 43)

1. Responding effectively to a telephone call takes practice. Telephone response is dependent upon words, since there are no visual cues. Face-to-face conversations are enhanced by body language and facial expression, but telephone conversations are dependent upon words alone.

2. Ask students whether or not they like to talk on the telephone.

3. Ask who they enjoy talking to on the telephone and why they enjoy those conversations.

4. Discuss the importance of response when talking on the telephone.

5. Ask for ideas on responses that keep conversation flowing. For example, if someone asks, "How you are?" it is helpful to the conversation to answer and then ask a question in return (e.g., "I'm fine. How are you?"). Point out that silence in a phone call can be uncomfortable and a signal to end the conversation.

6. Choose two students to role-play different conversations.

7. Direct students to keep a log of their telephone conversations during the week in their journals (page 43) and note whom the conversations were with and whether or not they were comfortable conversations. Instruct them to note what made certain conversations comfortable or uncomfortable.

8. Tell the students that when their journals are complete, the class will determine what responses made conversation most comfortable.

The Big Switch

1. Explain to the students that people use different verbal expressions, voice tones, and vocabulary when speaking with different types of people.

2. Ask two students to demonstrate how they would talk with friends on the telephone. Then have them contrast this to the way they would speak to strangers or professionals.

3. For each modeled conversation, discuss the amount of information shared, the degree of formality in words, and the length of the conversations. Tell students that this is *code switching* and that it is important to use a conversation style appropriate to the person and situation of each telephone call.

Conflict Resolution

Children are quite able to resolve their own relationship conflicts if given the opportunity and a bit of instruction.

Talking It Through

Objective: Students often need a bit of guidance to help them express their feelings and work out their problems.

1. When two children have a conflict, take them aside and ask them each to tell you, briefly, about the problem.

2. Ask child #1 to tell you the main thing about which he or she is upset. Then instruct the student to tell child #2 in simple terms, such as "I'm upset because…."

3. Then ask child #2, "How do you feel about this?" Have this child respond in a simple statement to child #1.

4. Continue by asking each student how he or she wants to resolve the problem.
   "How would you like to see this problem worked out?"

5. Allow both students to respond by speaking their words to each other (not to you).

6. Once your students have had the opportunity to go through this process a few times, they will be better able to talk out their problems without your assistance.

7. If desired, use the form below for assistance with conflict resolution. Two students experiencing a conflict complete a copy of the form and then meet together to discuss their feelings. Encourage them to refer to the form if they need reminders of the points they wanted to include in the resolution.

Resolution Form

Explain your conflict. _____

_____

_____

What is the main thing you are upset about?

_____

_____

How would you like this conflict to be resolved?

_____

_____

Complete this sentence using the student's name at the beginning.
_____, I'm upset because _____

_____

Complete the remaining sentences.
I want you to _____
Here's how I would like this to be resolved: _____
Use this form to help you as you discuss the problem with your classmate. Ask the teacher for help if you need it. _____

_____

Personal Questions

Directions: Use the prompts below to assist you in asking personal questions of people you know. Write questions on the lines. Then ask the questions of someone you choose.

Questions about the person's day:

_____

_____

_____

Questions about family:

_____

_____

_____

Questions about hobbies:

_____

_____

_____

Questions about likes and dislikes:

_____

_____

_____

Questions about where he or she came from:

_____

_____

_____

Questions about friends:

_____

_____

_____

Questions about fears:

_____

_____

_____

Questions about problems or concerns:

_____

_____

_____

Solve the Mystery

Directions: As your teacher reads a mystery story, write down the questions you think of as you ponder the solution to the mystery. Answer these questions based on the information in the story.

Name of mystery story: _____

What clues do you have?

Clue #1: _____

Clue #2: _____

Clue #3: _____

Clue #4: _____

Clue #5: _____

What questions do you have about the clues? _____

_____

What questions do you have about the people/characters? _____

_____

What questions do you have about events? _____

_____

Who in the story makes you suspicious? _____

_____

What are your ideas about solving the mystery? Write a paragraph about it. _____

_____

_____

_____

_____

Scenario Cards

Directions: Duplicate and cut apart the cards. Use them with the "Code Switching" activity on page 30.

You are invited to go with your best friend's family on a weekend trip on a houseboat.

✳ What will you say to your friend's parents when they ask you?

✳ What will you say to your friend?

At an art gallery, you see a painting that you really don't like.

✳ What would you say about it to your friend?

✳ What would you say about it to the artist?

You are looking forward to your baseball game on Saturday. When you wake up, it's raining. Your mom tells you the game is cancelled.

✳ What will you say to your mom?

✳ What will you say to your teammates?

You are at your friend's house for dinner. Your friend's mom cooked dinner, and it tastes terrible.

✳ What will you say when your friend's mom asks why you aren't eating?

✳ What will you say to your own mom when she asks why you're hungry when you get home?

You have been nominated for student-body president.

✳ What will you say to the principal?

✳ What will you say to your teacher?

✳ What will you say to your friends?

You fall down and skin your knee.

✳ What do you say in front of your friends?

✳ What do you say in front of your family?

You got a perfect score on your math test. Your friend's dad congratulates you.

✳ What will you say to your friend's dad?

✳ What will you say to your friend?

You are about to go on a really scary ride at the fair.

✳ What do you say to your family about it?

✳ What do you say to your friends about it?

You want the playground at your school to be cleaned up.

✳ How will you talk about this to your friends?

✳ How will you talk about this to your principal?

You are with your little brother at a haunted house.

✳ What do you say to your little brother?

✳ What are you thinking to yourself?

Sentence Cards

Directions: Duplicate and cut apart the cards. Use them with the "Emotional Response Charade" activity on page 31.

This is a new guitar.	I saw the candle flicker.
There is a carnival at the park.	It's time to go.
That's a nice basket.	I hear music.
Look in the mirror.	I hear someone coming.
I hear something.	I think the train is coming.
What's that in the garage?	There's something under the dirt.
Did you see that?	It's a new computer.
I hear thunder.	The house was just painted.
Look at that dog.	Look at the sunset.
I see lots of clouds.	Give me your phone number.
Where's the vacuum?	Did you hear that?
I found a pair of shoes.	I saw that movie.
Don't yell.	There are so many flowers.
Are you friends with her?	It was such a strange day.
The wind is blowing.	I see something green.

Spinner

Directions: Duplicate the spinner wheel below. Insert a brass fastener through the center dot. Then attach a paperclip to the fastener to serve as a spinner. Use the spinner with the "Emotional Response Charade" activity on page 31.

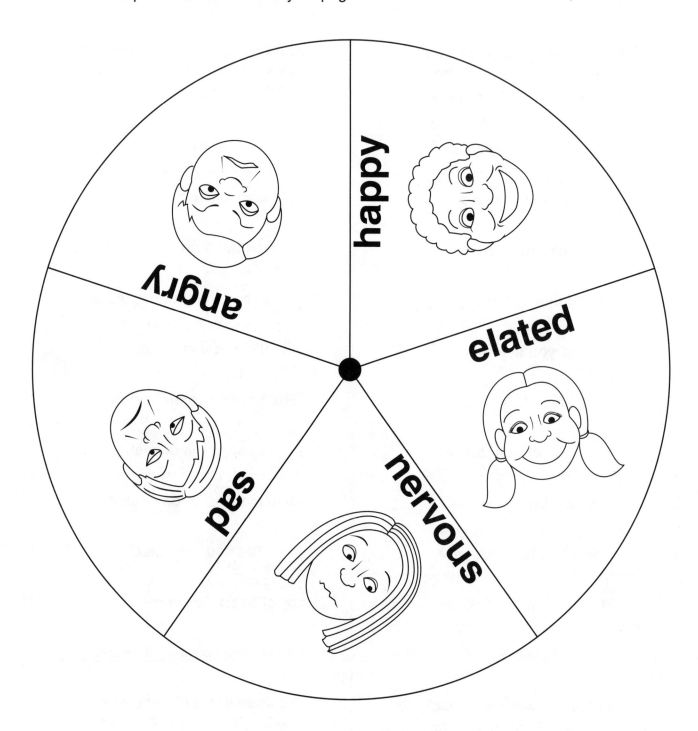

Charade Cards

Directions: Duplicate and cut apart the cards. Use with the "Response Charades" activity on page 32.

You have fallen down and you need help getting up off the ground.	You begin to brush your teeth and realize you don't have toothpaste. Where is it?
You are having trouble picking up a very heavy box.	You are a kindergarten teacher and you are trying to keep all of your kids in line.
You have lost your glasses and you are having trouble finding them.	You are a parent trying to teach his/her kids to look both ways before crossing the street.
You are a mother trying to wake your child up for school.	You have something in your eye and you want someone to help you get it out.
You are a dog and you have lost your favorite toy.	You are baking cookies and you realize that you need a cup of sugar.
You are a baby bird that is nervous about flying from the nest for the first time. You want help from your mother and father.	You begin to sing a song and realize you have lost your voice.

Telephone Conversation Scenarios

Directions: Duplicate and cut apart the cards. Use with the "What Is Appropriate?" activity on page 33.

telephone call to the doctor	two friends planning activities for a Saturday morning
a conversation between teacher and parent	a child talking with a stranger who is asking if a parent is home
conversation between teacher and student	a call to a store asking if they carry a particular item
a call to the police	a call to a movie theater asking what movies are showing
a telephone call to a friend	a call to a friend to tell him or her good news
a call to the parent of a friend	a call to a coach asking about an upcoming game
a child asking a parent for permission	a conversation with your mom's friend
a call to order take-out food from a restaurant	a call to a friend about homework

Telephone Etiquette Journal

Directions: Duplicate a page for each student. Use with the "What Is Appropriate?" activity on pages 33 and the "Telephone Responses" activity on page 34.

Caller	Topic of Conversation	Comfortable?	Why?

Fluency

Fluency refers to a child's ability to read quickly with minimal errors. Fluent readers have the ability to do the following:

- recognize words quickly
- connect ideas in print to prior knowledge

- draw meaning from print
- read with little effort
- read with expression

Independent Silent Reading

Objective: This method involves many opportunities for students to read silently on their own. It is believed that repeated and monitored oral reading is the most effective way to assist children with fluency development. This is not a case, however, for the traditional "round-robin" reading, where children take turns reading aloud. Aside from the anxiety that round-robin reading can bring about with some children, it also only involves the one-time reading of small portions of text. Proper fluency instruction involves the repeated reading of relatively simple passages and the modeling of reading (pauses and expression) by more proficient readers.

Time and Again

Objective: When given the opportunity to read passages several times, students increase fluency. Fluency improves even more when students listen to fluent readers and then repeat the same passages. Remember that when working on fluency, students should be reading passages at or slightly below their reading levels.

1. Begin by explaining to the students that reading smoothly is an important skill.
2. Select a passage of text to read aloud to the students. Read in a choppy manner, pausing between words.
3. Ask the students to respond to the way you read the passage. Was it easy to understand? Was it enjoyable to listen to?
4. Tell the students that they will have the opportunity to listen to you read and then repeat the reading to practice fluency.
5. Begin by allowing the students to look through the passage and read it silently.
6. Then read aloud the first two sentences and have the students read it aloud afterward. Continue in this manner through the entire passage of text.
7. Draw students' attention to the way they are able to read smoothly when copying you.

Fluency *(cont.)*

Developing Character

Objective: Part of fluency involves reading with expression. Good readers use expression when reading any text aloud. They also change their expression when reading the words of a particular character. This activity will assist your students learn to read with expression.

1. Introduce a story with lots of dialog and distinctly different characters, such as *Bunnicula* by Deborah and James Howe.
2. Explain to the students that this is a story that is told by the family sheepdog.
3. Ask the students to think about how a sheepdog might sound if it were able to speak our language.
4. Tell the students that there are other characters in the story who speak, such as members of the dog's family and the family cat.
5. Begin reading the story, drawing attention to the different characters. Be sure to vary your voice from character to character to model the use of expression.
6. Encourage the students to borrow the book from you during free time to practice reading parts of the story using expression.

Recorded Voices

Objective: Encourage your students to take responsibility for their fluency development.
Materials: tape recorder with microphone, passage of text, copies of "Evaluating Fluency" (page 48)

1. Provide a tape recorder and a microphone at a learning center. This learning center should be situated in a relatively quiet area of the classroom.
2. Instruct a student to select a passage of text at an appropriate reading level. The student should practice reading the passage several times.
3. Then the child records himself or herself reading the passage.
4. Finally, have the child listen to the tape recording. Ask the child to evaluate his or her reading and determine areas of improvement.
5. Duplicate copies of "Evaluating Fluency" (page 48) to guide the students as they evaluate their fluency.

Class News

Objective: This activity engages the students as reporters.

1. Invite a guest speaker to visit the class to share about how a newscast is put together; or, if possible, visit a local television station and watch a newscast being taped.
2. Tell the class that they will be gathering and reporting news stories in class in order to create a class newscast.
3. As a class, brainstorm ideas for suitable stories, including those about weather and sports.
4. Direct each student to research a story and to write the story on a sheet of paper.
5. Assign each student a partner to assist in peer editing.
6. Allow time for the students to practice reading their stories so that they are fluent.
7. Perform the class newscast, having each student read aloud his or her story.

Fluency *(cont.)*

Invention Connection

Objective: This activity combines creative energy and writing as students create journals of their inventions.

1. Bring a collection of discarded materials to class, such as bits of wire, pieces of broken appliances, string, empty cans, paper-towel tubes, etc.
2. Tell the students that inventions are created from the imaginations of the inventors and are often initially made from odds and ends that the inventors put together.
3. Show some examples of inventions, such as an apple-core remover, a corn-cob holder, a postage-stamp holder, a candle snifter, etc. Ask students to guess the use of each item.
4. Instruct students to brainstorm devices that they would like to invent.
5. Ask each student to sketch the idea.
6. Distribute the materials on a table and have the students create their devices.
7. Direct each student to write a description of his or her device, explaining it as thoroughly as possible.
8. After all students have completed their written descriptions, have them practice reading them several times to improve reading fluency.
9. Then direct each to present his or her device to the class.

> **Extension:** Collect discarded objects from the schoolyard and from students' homes to use for the inventions.

Read to a Friend

Objective: Reading to an audience is an incentive for reading with fluency. While a large audience can be intimidating, reading to a friend and being read to by a friend can be a rewarding experience.

1. Provide an assortment of age-appropriate books and magazines.
2. Instruct students to choose reading partners.
3. Direct each student to select a book or magazine of interest.
4. Ask each student to read his or her selection in order to locate something to share with his or her partner. Sharing should include reading to the other person and discussing the selection together.
5. Ask for volunteers to read their selections to the class.

> **Extensions:**
> 1. Have your students read to a class of younger students. Older students should be responsible for selecting material that would be interesting to the youngsters.
> 2. Tape-record readings for use in listening centers for younger children.
> 3. Instruct pairs of students to create a Reader's Theater performance of their selections.

Fluency *(cont.)*

A Personal Moment

Objective: Fluency often comes more readily when relating a personal experience. Have each student write about an event that made an impact on his or her life and then read the narrative to others.

1. Provide an example of a personal experience.

2. Tell the students why this experience had such an impact on your life that you still remember many details.

3. Direct students to brainstorm such events. Topics could include the following:

   ➤ a most frightening experience

   ➤ a most important experience

   ➤ something that made them very proud, very happy, or very sad

4. Instruct the students to think of personal experiences they can remember very clearly and write about them. Direct them to include as many details as possible.

5. Instruct each student to read his or her story to an editing partner.

6. Direct the editing partners to offer suggestions for clarity and understanding.

7. Instruct the partners to switch roles and offer suggestions one another.

8. Have students edit their stories.

9. Ask for volunteers to read their stories to the class.

Scavenger Hunt

Objective: This activity consists of the oral reading of portions of a book that the class has just finished reading.

Materials: student copies of a book selection, student copies of "Plot Line" (page 49)

1. To prepare students, begin with a class review of the book.

2. Ask the students to remember the sequence of events that occurred in the story.

3. Then draw a line on the chalkboard and ask for volunteers to create a plot line by writing story events in order along the line. (See page 49 for an example. You can provide copies of the plot-line page to students and have them complete the page with events from the story.)

4. Read aloud random passages from the book and direct students to locate the passages. The first student (or pair of students) to find the passage should read the surrounding paragraph aloud to the class.

5. Continue reading passages until the book has been thoroughly reviewed and most students have had a chance to read aloud.

Reading in Pairs

Objective: Paired student reading is another way that students can practice fluency.

Materials: student copies of a book selection, student copies of "Reading in Pairs" (page 50)

1. Think about combinations of students who you think will work well together. You may wish to choose mixed-ability groups so that a struggling reader can hear a fluent reader.

2. Instruct students to set common goals and work together to read with fluency.

3. Provide students with copies of the form on page 50.

4. After each partner reading, each student should complete the form.

Evaluating Fluency

Directions: Practice reading a passage of text. Ask for help with reading any words that are unfamiliar to you. Record your voice as you read the passage. Complete the top part of this page to evaluate your reading fluency.

Date:_____

Name of passage: _____

My reading was   **very smooth**   **somewhat smooth**   **choppy**.

My reading rate was   **too fast**   **too slow**   **just right**.

I made mistakes reading these words: _____

_____

Did I use expression?   **Yes**   **No**

Here is my plan for improvement: _____

_____

_____

_____

_____

Practice reading the passage and then record yourself again. Then complete the evaluation again.

My reading was   **very smooth**   **somewhat smooth**   **choppy**.

My reading rate was   **too fast**   **too slow**   **just right**.

I made mistakes reading these words: _____

_____

Did I use expression?   **Yes**   **No**

Here is how my reading fluency changed: _____

_____

_____

_____

_____

Plot Line

Directions: Use with the "Scavenger Hunt" activity on page 47. Remember the sequence of events that occurred in a story. Write story events in order along the line.

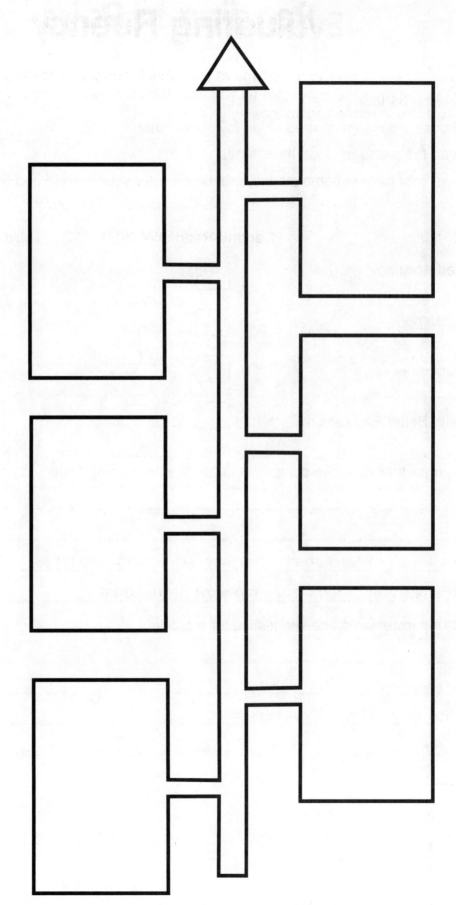

Reading in Pairs

Directions:

1. Select a partner.
2. Choose a passage to read aloud to your partner.
3. Read the passage aloud three times.
4. Have your partner complete the form below after your second and third readings.

	Second Reading	**Third Reading**
Improved Accuracy	☐	☐
Read Faster	☐	☐
Read Smoother	☐	☐
Read with Better Expression	☐	☐

Have your partner write two compliments about your reading fluency.

_____

_____

_____

_____

Have your partner write one suggestion for practice.

_____

_____

_____

_____

Four-Point Rubric

Use this rubric to assist with assessing your students' fluency progress.

4	The student reads with appropriate phrasing. Very few mistakes are made and do not take away from the meaning of the passage. The student reads expressively throughout all or most of the passage.
3	The student generally reads with appropriate phrasing. Some mistakes are made with word pronunciation. The student attempts to read with expression.
2	The student reads in two- to four-word phrases. Some word-pronunciation mistakes are made. The student does not read with expression.
1	The student reads word by word, makes frequent mistakes in pronunciation, and does not use expression.

The Power of Persuasion

The following activities will assist your students in developing and sharing their opinions.

Developing Opinions

Objective: There is an art to persuasion, and developing an opinion is the first step.

Materials: copies of "Sharing Your Opinion" (page 54)

1. Ask students if they have ever tried to convince someone to do something or to let them do something.
2. As they share, write their responses on the chalkboard.
3. Explain that in order to persuade someone, it is important to develop a strong opinion about the topic.
4. Write the following controversial statements on the chalkboard:
   ➤ Kids should spend weekends doing homework.
   ➤ Kids should not be given any allowance.
   ➤ Pizza should be served for lunch every day.
   ➤ When kids misbehave at school, classmates should determine the consequences.
   ➤ Recess should not be a part of the school day.
5. As you read each statement aloud, encourage the students to develop an opinion.
6. Next, divide the class into small groups. Provide students with copies of "Sharing Your Opinion." Instruct each group to select a controversial statement for which they all share the same opinion.
7. Have the group write a statement expressing its opinion, as well as reasons supporting this opinion.
8. Encourage group members to practice reciting their statements in preparation for oral presentations to the class.

Disagreeing in a Nice Way

Objective: Not everyone agrees with our opinions, so it's important that students know how to respond to those who disagree.

1. Begin the lesson by making a controversial statement, such as, "I think all classrooms should be absolutely quiet all day."
2. Allow the students to react to this bold statement.
3. Discuss with the students that people have differing opinions about different issues. It is important to be kind and polite when disagreeing with someone.
4. Explain that people have different ways of reacting to those who disagree with them. Some people attack, which means they say harsh things. Some people get upset and become sad or get their feelings hurt.
5. Ask the students to think of the best way to handle a situation where they don't agree with another person's opinion.

The Power of Persuasion *(cont.)*

Disagreeing in a Nice Way *(cont.)*

6. Provide the following tips for students:

   ☞ Ask the person to clarify his or her opinion.

   ☞ Ask for reasons why the person feels this way.

   ☞ Acknowledge the person's opinion and then express yours.

   ☞ Provide reasons for why you hold this opinion.

7. Explain that by asking a person to clarify an opinion, they will gain understanding of the person. For example, with the statement, "I think all classrooms should be absolutely quiet all day," a person might say, "I feel this way because I don't want kids to have fun at school" or "I feel this way because I think kids should be able to work without being disturbed." These two responses provide greater insight.

8. Next, explain that acknowledging someone's opinion means to recognize this opinion or accept the person's right to have this opinion. It does not mean that you have to agree. When you acknowledge a person's opinion, you might say, "I understand why you feel that way, but my opinion is…"

9. Finally, explain that it is important to provide reasons for your opinion.

10. Using the original statement from step 1, ask for volunteers to question you about this opinion and then to present theirs.

Commercial Persuasion

Objective: This activity helps your students to understand the use of persuasion in advertising.

Materials: video recording of TV commercials, copies of "Creative Advertisements" (page 55)

1. Begin the lesson by discussing commercials the students have seen on television. Ask them what is the purpose of these advertisements.

2. Explain that companies try very hard to sell their products. It is important for them to get your attention and present their products in a way that persuades you to buy it.

3. Show several television commercials. Draw students' attention to the words used in the commercials and the expressive tone of voice used by the people in the advertisements.

4. Read the following text using a monotone voice with no expression.

   Gina's Pizza has the best pizza in town. You'll love every bite of its spicy taste. Gina's Pizza is a great place for families. There is music for the grownups and plenty of fun for the kids. So, come on over to Gina's Pizza. We're waiting for you!

5. Ask what was wrong with this advertisement. Then read the text again, this time using plenty of expression.

6. Ask the students to compare the two readings. Which one was more persuasive? Point out that expression is extremely important in advertising.

7. Divide the class into small groups to create an oral advertisement for a fictitious product or store. Provide copies of page 55 for assistance. Encourage students to use persuasive words and expression.

8. Allow groups to present their advertisements to the class.

Sharing Your Opinion

Directions: Think about an important issue. Write it on the line below. Then write your opinion and your reasons for this opinion. Complete the remainder of the page. Use with the "Developing Opinions" activity on page 52.

Issue: _____

Opinion: _____

_____

Reasons supporting opinion:

1. _____

2. _____

3. _____

4. _____

5. _____

Why should others feel the same way? _____

_____

_____

_____

Write a statement including the information above.

_____

_____

_____

_____

_____

_____

_____

Creative Advertisements

Directions: Use with "Commercial Persuasion" on page 53. Create an oral advertisement for a make-believe product or store. Don't forget to use persuasive words and expression.

Name of product, store, or restaurant: _____

Expressive words that describe the product or store:

_____

_____

_____

_____

_____

_____

What is great about this product, store, or restaurant?

_____

_____

Who would be interested in this?

_____

_____

What should be the tone of your commercial—excited, peaceful, etc.?

_____

Write the words of your commercial below.

_____

_____

_____

_____

_____

_____

Books, Movies, Events

It is helpful to hear about a book before reading it, to know what a movie is about before seeing it, or to know what an event entails before spending time and often money to attend it. The following activities will assist your students in writing and presenting reviews.

What's Your Favorite?

Objective: This activity is designed to help students discern whether the information about a book, movie, or event is based on fact or opinion and how credible the recommendation might be.

Materials: favorite book, movie review from a newspaper, copies of "Writing a Review" (page 58)

1. Bring a copy of a favorite book to class. Show it to the students and tell them that it is the best book ever.

2. Ask the students whether this is a fact or an opinion.

3. Talk about the difference between a fact and an opinion, asking for examples of each.

4. Ask the students whether knowing that you like the book makes any of them want to read it or whether they need more information to decide whether or not they want to read it.

5. Read a movie review from the newspaper.

6. Ask the students to determine whether the review is based on facts about the movie or on the opinion of the reviewer.

7. Lead students to realize that a stronger review is based on facts about the movie, book, or event, rather than on the opinion of a reviewer.

8. Brainstorm with the students, criteria for a strong review. List their suggestions on the chalkboard.

9. Provide each student with a copy of page 58. Direct students to think of a favorite book, movie, or event and to write a review of it.

10. Have students practice reading their reviews aloud before sharing them with the rest of the class. Determine whether each is based on fact or opinion.

Coffeehouse Book Sharing

Objective: This activity provides an opportunity for students to share books that they have read in an interesting setting.

1. Introduce this lesson by bringing several books to class and showing them to the students while sharing a few interesting thoughts about each one.

2. Ask the students to think of a few books that they have read and enjoyed.

3. Invite the students to bring a few favorite books to class with them on a designated day and be prepared to share them with the rest of the class. Suggest that they tell a little bit about the books and read a few paragraphs.

4. To create a coffeehouse setting, set up your classroom with tables, tablecloths, dimmed lights, candles, light music, etc. Serve drinks and light snacks.

5. Then have each student present his or her book review to the class.

6. Provide paper and pencils on the tables so that classmates can write titles that sound interesting to them as the books are shared.

Books, Movies, Events *(cont.)*

Creating Reviews

Objective: This activity is designed to provide students practice in reviewing a book, movie, or event and writing recommendations for others.

Materials: copies of book, movie, and event reviews, "Writing a Review" (page 58)

1. Bring several reviews of movies, books, or events to class.

2. Read them aloud and ask whether or not any of the students are familiar with them. Ask whether or not they agree with the reviews. Do the reviews make them more interested?

3. Ask what part of the review was the most influential in making them want to read/see/experience it.

4. Tell the students that it is sometimes difficult for younger children to choose a book from the library and that having book reviews available might help them.

5. Instruct the students to use the "Writing a Review" (page 58) to write reviews of books for children in first and second grades.

6. Take the class to the library and direct each student to choose a book to review for younger students. Tell them that it can be a book that they enjoyed when they were younger or a new one that they can read and write a review about later.

7. When they have finished writing and editing the book reviews, direct the students to make a final copy to be bound into a class book for the library.

Class Newspaper

Objective: Class newspapers can provide practice for writing and presenting reviews of classroom and school events.

Materials: "Class News" (page 59), newspaper reviews of community events

1. Bring to class several newspaper reviews of community events.

2. Read the reviews to the students and ask how many students attended the events and whether the reviews seemed accurate.

3. Discuss the format for the reviews and whether or not the format could be applied to reviews of school events.

4. Brainstorm some events that could be reviewed.

5. Have students work in small groups to write reviews for the various events.

6. Include completed review on the "Class News" form on page 59.

7. Allow students to visit other classrooms, presenting copies of their newspaper and giving oral presentations of the reviews contained in it.

Writing a Review

Directions: Write a review of a book, movie, or event.

Name of the book, movie, or event: _____

Author (if applicable): _____

Name of the reviewer: _____

Type of book, movie, or event: _____

How it began: _____

_____

_____

_____

One or two parts that were especially interesting: _____

_____

_____

Was it exciting? Explain. _____

_____

_____

_____

Did you like it? Explain. _____

_____

_____

_____

_____

Recommendation: **Yes** ☐   **No** ☐

Class News

Directions: Use with the "Class Newspaper" activity on page 57. Students write reviews in the sections below.

_____

(*headline*)

_____   _____
(*book, movie, event*)   (*book, movie, event*)

Review by_____   Review by_____

_____   _____

_____   _____

_____   _____

_____   _____

_____   _____
(*book, movie, event*)   (*book, movie, event*)

Review by_____   Review by_____

_____   _____

_____   _____

_____   _____

_____   _____

Storytelling

Oral communication can consist of formal speaking experiences, but it can also involve informal experiences like storytelling. It is important that your students understand that they have stories to tell.

Daily Routine

Objective: Develop a daily routine of informal storytelling in your classroom.

1. At the beginning of every day—after attendance, lunch count, and all of the morning routine—allow your students to tell stories.

2. Begin by saying, "Does anyone have anything to share?" Stress the importance of listening. This will take a little bit of time, but the students will soon realize that they will all have their chance to tell a story and that everyone will listen to them when they do.

3. Inevitably, you see that one story leads to another and another on the same topic.

4. Storytelling does not always have to be about personal experiences. Learning to create stories orally is a valuable skill, as well.

5. Learn more about storytelling by performing an Internet search on the topic. Use search terms, such as "storytelling" or "storytelling activities." You're sure to find many useful Web sites that will provide more insight and ideas for storytelling with young children.

Retelling Fairy Tales

Objective: Begin imaginative storytelling by having students retell familiar fairy tales with their own embellishments.

Materials: short fairy tales

1. Read aloud a few familiar fairy tales to the students.

2. Draw the students' attention to the characters, their personalities, the settings, and events.

3. Group students into pairs and have them take turns retelling favorite fairy tales.

4. Encourage them to think about the characters in the tale and include details describing the characters and events that take place in the story.

5. Allow the student to embellish their stories with their own new characters and new situations added.

Picture This

Objective: Use photographs and paintings to inspire students' storytelling experiences.

Materials: photographs, paintings, pictures from books and/or magazines

1. Select a photograph or painting to show the children.

2. Ask the students to think about the story they think the image tells.

3. Encourage them to offer their ideas.

4. Then determine a general idea for the story and ask the students to dictate sentences to tell the story as you write their words on the chalkboard.

Storytelling *(cont.)*

The Five W's Group Story

Objective: This activity is designed to provide practice in story organization through the Five W's.

Materials: short story

1. The Five W's are essential to every story. Being able to identify who, what, where, when, and why as they occur in a story helps comprehension and is essential to composition.

2. Explain to the students that all stories have five components known as the Five W's.

3. Write the Five W's (who, what, where, when, why) on the chalkboard.

4. Tell or read a short story to the class.

5. Direct students to identify each of the Five W's from the story.

6. Divide the class into groups of five. There should be one student in each group for each of the Five W's.

7. Direct each group to meet for 15 minutes to develop a story to tell the class that includes all of the Five W's. Each member is responsible to provide his or her designated topic.

8. Gather the class together to tell the stories.

A Long Time Ago...

Objective: This activity is designed to spark an interest in local history and extend that history into the present.

1. History can be very interesting to students when they feel connected to events.

2. Invite someone who has lived in the local area for a long time to speak to the class about local history as they remember it.

3. Invite students to ask questions of the speaker after he or she has finished.

4. After the speaker has left, gather the students in a circle and tell them that they will create a group story that takes place in the community many years ago. The story should be based on what they have learned from the speaker.

5 Give one student a ball of yarn and direct him or her to hold the yarn and begin telling the story. When finished, the student holds the yarn and tosses the ball to another student who continues the story. After that student is ready for someone else to continue the story, he or she holds onto the string of yarn and tosses the ball to another student.

6. Continue in this manner until every student is holding a piece of the yarn and has contributed to the story. Draw their attention to the yarn web created by the storytelling experience.

7. Close by asking for comments as to whether the students would like to have lived at the time when the story took place.

Extension: Use this activity as a follow-up to reading an historic novel or studying a unit in social studies.

Storytelling *(cont.)*

The Family Story Tree

Objective: Family stories are especially meaningful to students and are rooted in the oral tradition. This activity is designed to help children retrace and share their family stories.

Materials: family tree pattern (page 74), a copy of your family tree (created from page 74)

1. Introduce the concept of a family tree by showing your own family tree.

2. Tell a story about one or two of the people represented on your family tree.

3. Distribute copies of page 74 to each student and direct each one to create a family tree using yours as a model.

4. Direct students to fill in as many names on their family trees as possible. Tell them that their homework assignment is to take their family trees home and ask their parents to provide the missing names and to tell them a few family stories.

5. Instruct the students to take notes about the stories that they are told and to be prepared to share a few in class.

6. The following day, ask for volunteers to share their family trees and family stories with the class.

> **Extension:** Divide the class into small groups and have students share their family trees and stories within a small group setting.

Tall Tales from the Classroom

Objective: Tall tales fascinate students and stimulate the imagination. This activity introduces the tall tale format and extends it into the classroom as students create their own tall tales.

Materials: tall-tale stories

1. Introduce tale-tales by reading or telling a few such stories (e.g., Paul Bunyon, Pecos Bill, Johnny Appleseed, or Casey Jones).

2. Tell students that most tall tales began with an actual person or event but were greatly exaggerated.

3. Ask students to guess what parts of the stories might have been accurate. For example, Paul Bunyon was probably a very large, strong man.

4. Direct students to find a partner and brainstorm ideas for creating a tall tale about themselves or someone that they know.

5. Instruct students to individually think of a characteristic of themselves or someone they know or of an event in their own lives that could be developed into a tall tale.

6. Have each student create an outline of the story. Tell students that tall tales were first shared orally, and let them know that they will tell their stories rather than write them.

7. Have students share their ideas with their partners and develop their outlines into a story that they will share with the class. Partners should provide feedback on clarity and sequencing.

8. Ask for volunteers to share their tall tales in front of the class.

Script Memorization and Performance

Script Comprehension

Objective: Before a script can be memorized, it needs to be thoroughly comprehended. This activity is designed to insure comprehension.

Materials: copies of dialog from a story, highlighter pen

1. Explain to the class that they will be memorizing the script for a play.
2. Begin by dividing the class into small groups. Provide each group with a copy of dialog from a selected book. (The dialog should have the same number of characters as group members.)
3. Direct the groups to assign character parts to each person.
4. Have each student use a highlighter pen to mark his or her dialog to read.
5. Instruct the groups to begin reading the dialog by having the readers first read the dialog, then paraphrase the words that they have read.
6. When all groups have read through the dialog and paraphrased the script, have them discuss its content.
7. Have the students rewrite the dialog in script form. Allow students to use either the dialog from the book selection or paraphrased dialog.

Character Development

Objective: In order for a play to be believable, the characters must seem real to the performers. It is not enough to read a character's words, but the performers must feel what the characters feel and do what the characters would do. This activity is designed to help students think about character development in order to make the play believable.

Materials: short story with dialog

1. Read aloud a short story that contains character dialog. Then list all characters on the chalkboard.
2. Direct the students to describe the way they perceive each character. Encourage them to talk about how the character looks, acts, talks, and moves.
3. Direct the students to close their eyes and picture each character in their minds.
4. Ask for volunteers to perform parts of the story, taking on the roles of the character and using the expressions and gestures of the characters.

Script Memorization and Performance *(cont.)*

Character Pantomime

Objective: This activity is designed to help students portray characters without using words.

Materials: play script (pages 75 and 76; or see page 68 for ideas)

1. Divide students into small groups. Provide each group with a script (see pages 75 and 76).
2. After each group reviews the script, have the students attempt to perform the play without the use of words. Explain that this can be done using exaggerated expressions, gestures, and body movements.
3. Ask the students to discuss the challenges they faced when trying to dramatize the script without the use of words.
4. Explain that actions portray meaning in much the same way as words do.

Script Memorization

Objective: After character parts have been assigned, the script needs to be memorized. Practice is the best way to accomplish memorization.

Materials: copies of scripts (pages 75 and 76; or see page 68 for ideas)

1. Assign a student to serve as a prompter. Provide this student with a copy of a play script or fable from a book such as *Fables* by Arnold Lobel.
2. Explain that the script must be memorized in order to deliver an effective performance.
3. Direct the students to read through the play using scripts.
4. After the first reading, direct students to try to say their parts without looking at the script. Encourage them to pay attention to what is happening in the play because this will help them remember their own parts.
5. Instruct the prompter to give a word or two if the person reading can't remember his or her lines.
6. Direct the students to read through the play several times in an effort to memorize their lines.

Acting with Actions

Objective: This activity is designed to help students to determine the action in the play.

Materials: script from a play or student-created scripts

1. It is important that students have ownership of their play. In order to achieve this goal, they should be in charge of as much of the production as possible.
2. Divide the class into groups and assign roles. Then read through the script together as a class, having students read their assigned parts.
3. Direct all students to visualize the action as the play is read.
4. Following the reading, ask individuals to share the actions they visualized as they listened to the play. Record their ideas on the chalkboard.
5. Discuss the ideas and sequence them.
6. Allow students time in class to meet with their groups to rehearse agreed-upon actions.

> **Extension:** Use the same procedures for generating student-made scenery, props, and costumes.

Script Memorization and Performance *(cont.)*

Performance Preparation

Objective: There is nothing as refreshing or entertaining as a school play. Some of the most effective performances are those where it is obvious that the students are enjoying the experience. Performance preparation must be relaxed and allow for flexibility.

1. Talk with the students about a play that they have seen. If possible, watch a play that is presented by another class.

2. Discuss the importance of delivering lines with volume and enunciation.

3. Discuss the importance of making actions large enough to be seen by the audience.

4. Remind the students that being part of a play is fun and that they should enjoy the experience.

5. Tell the students that it is important to keep the play moving.

6. Talk through what to do if they forget their lines. Practice a few scenarios so that they feel prepared for anything that might happen.

7. Remind them to have fun and help the audience to enjoy watching the play.

Porquois Stories for the Classroom

Objective: Porquois stories are used to explain the reason things happen, such as, "Why I'm Afraid of Thunder" or "Why Snow Falls from the Sky." Tap into students' desire to explain the unknown as they create their own porquois stories patterned after this genre of folk tale.

Materials: stories such as "Rainbow Crow" by Nancy Van Laan or "Why Mosquitoes Buzz in People's Ears" by Verna Aardema.

1. Read a few examples of stories that tell why something happened or how something came to be the way it is. Examples could include some of the traditional porquois tales or books, such as "Rainbow Crow" by Nancy Van Laan or "Why Mosquitoes Buzz in People's Ears" by Verna Aardema.

2. Ask students whether or not these are true explanations and discuss their answers.

3. Ask students what makes them good stories.

4. Brainstorm several subjects that they could create stories about. Examples might include the following:

   ➢ Why the squirrel has a bushy tale

   ➢ Why trees lose their leaves

   ➢ Why it thunders during a storm

5. Divide the class into groups and assign each group a topic for a tale.

6. Direct the groups to brainstorm a story to tell to the rest of the class and write an outline so they remember the story and the sequence of events. Tell students that these tales will be presented orally rather than written.

7. Ask for volunteers to share their stories.

Reader's Theater

Creating Reader's Theater

Objective: Reader's theater is a wonderful way for students to share a story together.

Materials: tape recorder with microphone, recording of an old radio show (e.g., *The Green Hornet, I Love A Mystery, The Shadow, The Lone Ranger*, etc.)

1. Introduce reader's theater to the class by playing a tape of an old radio program that used a reader's theater format. Examples of these programs include *The Green Hornet, I Love A Mystery, The Shadow*, and *The Lone Ranger*.

2. Select a favorite story with which the entire class is familiar.

3. Tell students that they will revise the story so that it becomes a reader's theater and then perform it as though it were a radio program.

4. Ask the students how a reader's theater story is different from a regular story.

5. Direct the students to think of the characters that are in the story. List them on the chalkboard.

6. Introduce the idea of a narrator and tell the students that everything that is not something that the characters say will be included in the narrator's part.

7. Go through the story and assign words to each of the characters in order to develop the story line in a script format.

8. Direct the whole class to read through the script that they have written.

9. Assign students to read parts, including the narrator. (It is important that everyone has a part to read; several students can read each part, if necessary.)

10. Read through the story again with each student reading his or her part.

11. Discuss the importance of inflection in order to communicate meaning. Tell the students that in reader's theater there are no actions to communicate meaning, so importance is placed on voices.

12. After several practice runs, perform the story into a tape recorder as if it were a radio program.

13. Play the tape back so students can listen to their reader's theater presentation.

Sound Effects

Objective: Reader's theater can be enhanced by sound effects. It is fun for students to use their imaginations to create sounds to accompany a story.

Materials: reader's theater script (see page 68), assorted items for sound effects

1. Direct the students to close their eyes and listen while you demonstrate several sound effects and ask them what the sounds remind them of.

2. Invite them to explore items around the classroom to determine the sounds they make and to think of how the sounds might be used to help tell a story.

3. Review a story written in a reader's theater format (see page 68) and brainstorm sound effects that might enhance the story.

4. Invite students to incorporate sound effects into the story and prepare it for performance.

Reader's Theater *(cont.)*

Voice Inflection

Objective: In order to be effective, the readers in a reader's theater production need to communicate meaning through voice inflection.

Materials: copies of passages from different stories, "Reader's Theater Planner" (page 77)

1. Ask for two volunteers to read the same passage from a story. Direct one reader to read the passage without voice inflection and the other reader to add voice inflection.

2. Discuss with the class how voice inflection makes a difference in communicating meaning.

3. Brainstorm various ways of reading a passage and ask for volunteers to demonstrate. For example, a reader could read as though he or she were in a hurry, frightened, excited, bored, etc.

4. Remind students that in reader's theater it is especially important to use correct voice inflection in order to communicate meaning.

5. Allow students to practice reading several passages with a variety of voice inflections.

6. Then have students work in groups to write their own reader's theater scripts. Encourage them to create parts for individual readers and for the group to read together.

7. Have students perform their reader's theaters using appropriate voice inflection.

Character Headbands

Objective: When performing reader's theater, the students often need a prop in order to make them feel more like the character that they are representing. In this activity, the students make headbands to use as props as they participate in the story.

Materials: story written in reader's theater format; paper strips, construction paper, markers

1. Tell the students that they are going to perform a story using their voices rather than actions.

2. Explain that since they will be seen by the audience, performers will wear headbands so that the audience will be able to identify the various characters.

3. Read through the story so that students know what the story is about and who the characters are.

4. Assign parts to the students.

5. Distribute materials for the headbands and direct each student to create one that is appropriate for his or her character.

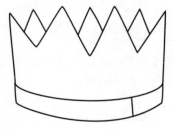

6. When students have completed their headbands, direct them to read through the story while wearing their headbands.

Reader's Theater

Are you looking for sources of scripts for plays and reader's theater? You can find many scripts online by using a search engine with the search term "reader's theater scripts." In addition to this, here's a collection of books to help get you started.

Blau, Lisa. *Fall Is Fabulous*!: *Reader's Theatre Scripts and Extended Activities.* One From the Heart, 1997.

Fredericks, Anthony D. *Frantic Frogs and Other Frankly Fractured Folktales for Readers Theatre.* Teacher Ideas Press, 1993.

Laughlin, Mildred Knight, Peggy Tubbs Black, and Margery Kirby Loberg. *Social Studies Readers Theatre for Children: Scripts and Script Development.* Teacher Ideas Press, 1991.

Laughlin, Mildred Knight, and Kathy Howard Latrobe. *Readers Theatre for Children: Scripts and Script Development.* Teacher Ideas Press, 1990.

McBride-Smith, Barbara. *Tell It Together: Foolproof Scripts for Story Theatre.* August House Publishers, 2001.

McCory Martin, Justin. *12 Fabulously Funny Fairy Tale Plays.* Instructor Books, 2002.

Shepard, Aaron. *Folktales on Stage: Children's Plays for Reader's Theater (or Readers Theatre), With 16 Play Scripts From World Folk and Fairy Tales and Legends, Including African, Chinese, Southeast Asian, Indian, Middle Eastern, Russian, Scandinavian, and Native American.*

————. *Readers on Stage: Resources for Reader's Theater (or Readers Theatre), with Tips, Play Scripts, and Worksheets.* Shepard Publications, 2004.

————. *Stories on Stage: Scripts for Reader's Theater.* H. W. Wilson, 1993.

Sierra, Judy. *Multicultural Folktales for the Feltboard and Readers' Theater.* Oryx Press, 1996.

White, Melvin R. *Mel White's Readers Theatre Anthology: A Collection of 28 Readings (Reader's Theater Series).* Meriwether Publishing, Ltd., 1993.

Wolf, Joan M. *Cinderella Outgrows the Glass Slipper and Other Zany Fractured Fairy Tale Plays.* Scholastic Professional Books, 2002.

Puppet Shows

Create a Puppet

Objective: Most children love to create things from interesting bits and pieces of materials. As they become involved in the process of creating, inhibitions fall away and they express themselves freely.

Materials: assorted materials, such as fabric, feathers, tissue paper, cardboard, paper bags, paper towel tubes, foam balls, etc.; scissors; glue

1. Provide students with a variety of interesting materials (see the materials list above).

2. Display several different types of puppets (or pictures of puppets) to the class to help introduce the lesson. Using different voices, let the puppets introduce themselves to the class and explain to the students that they will be making more puppets to use in puppet shows.

3. Direct the students to select materials that they want to use to make puppets.

4. If desired, play some lively music as they work for inspiration.

5. When puppets are completed, invite each student to introduce his or her puppet to the class and tell one thing about it. Encourage them to use interesting voices as they speak for the puppets.

Creative Puppet Making

Objective: Have your students make different kinds of puppets to inspire performances.

* **Paper Bag Puppets**

  1. Have each student slip his or her hand inside a paper lunch bag, with fingers curling aroun the folded portion of the base of the bag.

  2. Show them that when they move their fingers, the folded portion of the bag moves. This will be the puppet's mouth.

  3. Provide a variety of craft materials and have each student create the upper portion of the puppet's face on the flap of the bag. The lower portion of the mouth is created just below the flap.

  4. Encourage each student to create an outfit and hair for the puppet as well.

* **Stick Puppets**

  1. Provide each student with a wooden craft stick and other craft materials, such as fabric, construction paper, sequins, etc.

  2. The student creates a puppet from the materials and then attaches it to the craft stick.

* **Simple Sock Puppets**

  The simple way to make a sock puppet is to provide each student with a sock and then allow him or her to use markers and craft materials to create a face on the foot of the sock and a body on the tube part of the sock.

Puppet Shows *(cont.)*

Creative Puppet Making (cont.)

✳ Glove Puppets

1. Provide each student with a glove (e.g., a white glove, a garden glove, or a latex cleaning glove).

2. The glove puppet can be created in a few different ways. The glove could represent one character with a face on the palm and the fingers as hair. Another way to use the glove is to have each finger of the glove represent a different character. Each finger of the glove is a character's entire body.

3. Provide craft materials and permanent ink markers and allow the students to be creative.

✳ Elaborate Sock Puppets

A more elaborate sock puppet includes a mouth that opens and closes.

1. To create a puppet, slip your hand into the sock. Imagine where the face of the puppet will be in the foot of the sock.

2. Remove your hand from the sock and cut a slit in the sock about halfway between the toe and the heel of the sock. The slit is where the mouth will be.

3. Place your hand back inside the sock with your fingers near the toe and your thumb near the heel. Open your hand to reveal the hole you cut in the sock. Examine the size of this cut space.

4. Cut a piece of fabric that will cover this space. (See illustration.)

5. Sew the edges of the fabric piece to the cut edges of the sock opening. This will complete the puppet's mouth.

6. Use assorted craft materials (including large wiggle eyes) to complete the puppet.

✳ Paper Plate Puppets

1. Provide each student with two paper plates and a craft stick.

2. Stack the plates with the plate bottoms facing outward. Staple them together along the outer edges.

3. Slide the craft stick between the plates and then glue or tape it into place.

4. The student then decorates a puppet face on one side of the attached plates.

5. Provide assorted craft materials for embellishments.

Puppet Shows *(cont.)*

Puppet Bios

Objective: Getting to know one's puppet is important in order to make that puppet "come to life" for the student. In this activity, students will get to know their puppets better by writing biographies for them and sharing them with the class.

Materials: copies of "Puppet Character Chart" (page 78)

1. Reintroduce your puppets to the students and create some biographical information to share about each one.
2. Tell students that they are to think of information that they could include in a biography for their puppets and to write that information on a puppet character chart (see page 78).
3. Distribute a chart to each student.
4. When students have completed their charts, ask for volunteers to share the information about their puppets.
5. Then have students introduce their puppets (in a creative puppet voice), using the information they included on the character charts.
6. Encourage classmates to comment on the puppet biographies and the students' introductions of them.

Writing Puppet Shows

Objective: Have your students work together to create scripts for puppet shows.

1. After they have created puppets, the students should be placed into groups of three or four.
2. Instruct the students to share their puppets and the puppets' personalities.
3. Then instruct the students to work together to think about a story with their puppets interacting.
4. Once each group has come up with a story idea, have them each create a script for a puppet show.
5. Allow the students plenty of time in class to rehearse their plays before presenting to the class.

Performing the Puppet Show

Objective: Performance is the publishing step of creating. In performance, words come alive and meaning is communicated.

1. Tell the students that performance is the final step in preparing a puppet show.
2. Remind the students that the meaning depends upon voice inflection, volume, and puppet action.
3. Remind the students that they need to pay attention to what other puppets say and keep the dialogue moving.
4. Remind the students that actions need to be large enough that the audience can see them.
5. Direct students to perform the play and have fun.

Reciting Poetry

Phrasing

1. Explain to the students that when reading poetry, it is necessary to use proper phrasing. Define phrasing as chunking together groups of words.

2. Demonstrate reading that does not utilize correct phrasing. Do this by reading the first stanza of a favorite poem. Here is an example. Be sure to pause at the designated places.

   There was an old [pause] woman who lived in [pause] a shoe.

   She had [pause] so many [pause] children [pause] she didn't know [pause] what to do.

3. Draw students' attention to the fact that the stanza is difficult to understand when read in this manner.

4. Next, read the stanza again, pausing only at the end of each line, as follows:

   There was an old woman who lived in a shoe.

   She had so many children she didn't know what to do.

5. Ask the students to explain the difference between the two readings of the stanza. They will likely say that the second reading was smooth and made more sense. Explain that the second reading utilized correct phrasing. The words were chunked together in a more meaningful way.

6. Point out to students that reading word-by-word also makes phrasing difficult to accomplish. Read the stanza again in a choppy, word-by-word manner. Draw their attention to the fact that this kind of reading is difficult to understand and not as pleasant to hear.

7. Provide each student with a short poem to recite.

8. Ask the students to read the poem silently and then try reading it aloud, focusing on correct phrasing. Instruct them to take notice of the way the words sound when they are read fluidly with pauses at the ends of the lines. Explain that pauses also take place briefly when commas are inserted in the lines of the poem.

9. Allow the students time in class to practice their poetry readings before performing them for the class.

10. Have students recite their poetry in public settings, including the following:

    ➢ parent events
    ➢ school assemblies
    ➢ morning announcements
    ➢ coffeehouse presentations

11. Refer to "Ideas for Public Performances" on page 8 for explanations of these performances and for more ideas.

72

Storytelling Planner

Directions: Use this page to plan a story that you will tell aloud to the class or a friend.

Is this story exciting, interesting, scary, etc.?

Why do you want to share this story?

Who is in the story?

When did this happen?

What happened first?

What happened next?

How did the story end?

Practice telling the story out loud before sharing it with the class. Use your notes on this page to help you tell the story.

Family Tree

Directions: Use this page with "The Family Story Tree" on page 62 to create a family tree.

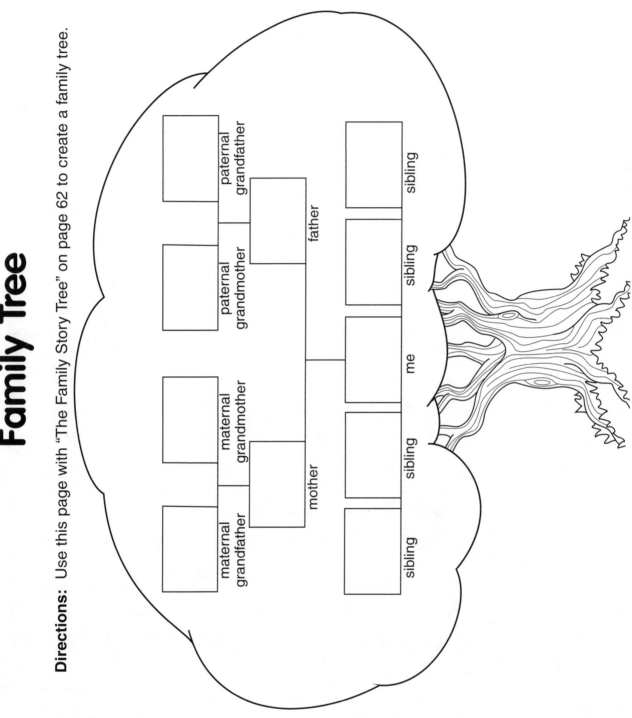

maternal grandfather

maternal grandmother

paternal grandmother

paternal grandfather

mother

father

sibling

sibling

me

sibling

sibling

Play Script

The Story of Chicken Pig

Characters	
Narrator	Farmer's wife
Farmer Johnson	Sophie

Narrator: For many years around the town of Shady Creek, folks talked about a very special pig named Chicken Pig. It all started when a litter of pigs was born at the Johnson's farm. Sophie Johnson was so excited with the tiny pink pigs that she could hardly stay out of the barn where they slept nestled up against their mother.

Sophie: Oh Dad, may I keep one for a pet?

Farmer Johnson: I think that might be a good idea, Sophie. You need to watch them all for about a week and then choose the one that you want to keep.

Narrator: Sophie watched the baby pigs for one week. They were already getting bigger and were making little sounds as they squirmed close to their mother's side.

Sophie: Dad, I think that I have chosen my favorite pig.

Farmer Johnson: Which one do you like the best, Sophie?

Sophie: I like the one with the white spot on its back. Is it a boy or a girl?

Farmer Johnson: It is a little girl—and a very good looking pig, if I do say so. Why don't you take her in to show your mother.

Sophie: Look, Mom, this is the pig that I have chosen to keep for a pet.

Farmer's wife: She is a very cute pig, Sophie. I like her white spot. What will you name her?

Sophie: I don't know yet. I need to get to know her and find a name that fits her just right.

Narrator: Six weeks went by, and soon it was time to find homes for the baby pigs. Sophie played with her pig every day and enjoyed watching the little pig explore the farm.

Narrator: Sophie kept her little pig very clean so that she could live in the house with the family. At night the little pig would curl up on a blanket beside Sophie's bed.

Farmer's wife: Your pig is getting pretty big, Sophie. Don't you think that she would rather sleep in the barn with the other animals?

Play Script *(cont.)*

The Story of Chicken Pig *(cont.)*

Sophie:	No, Mom. She likes to sleep in the house close to me. She would miss me if she were in the barn.
Narrator:	One day Sophie and her pig were playing outside when the pig disappeared. Sophie looked around but couldn't find her pig. She didn't know that her pig had found some mud and was having a wonderful time rolling around in it. After rolling in the mud, the pig went into the hen house and began chasing the chickens. That was when Sophie heard the noise and ran toward the hen house.
Sophie:	Mom, Dad, come here!
Farmer's wife:	What is it, Sophie?
Farmer Johnson:	What is wrong?
Sophie:	I can't find my pig, and there is a terrible noise coming from the hen house!
Narrator:	Farmer Johnson, his wife, and Sophie all stared at the hen house as the strangest creature emerged. The creature was not very big and was covered with chicken feathers. Although they had never seen anything like it, there was something sort of familiar about the strange-looking animal. Sophie was the first to recognize the two eyes that peered out from the feathers.
Sophie:	Look, Mom and Dad! My pig has become a chicken pig! I finally know what I will call her.
Narrator:	From that day on, the Johnson's pet pig was known around the town as Chicken Pig. Through the years, one of her favorite things to do was to roll in the mud and chase the chickens.

adapted from a story by Jack Dustman

Reader's Theater Planner

Directions: Use this page to write your reader's theater script. Be sure to include lines for the whole group to read together.

Reader 1: _____

Reader 2: _____

Reader 3: _____

Reader 4: _____

Reader 5: _____

All: _____

Reader 1: _____

Reader 2: _____

Reader 3: _____

Reader 4: _____

Reader 5: _____

All: _____

Reader 1: _____

Reader 2: _____

Reader 3: _____

Reader 4: _____

Reader 5: _____

All: _____

Reader 1: _____

Reader 2: _____

Reader 3: _____

Reader 4: _____

Reader 5: _____

All: _____

Reader 1: _____

Reader 2: _____

Reader 3: _____

Reader 4: _____

Reader 5: _____

All: _____

Puppet Character Chart

Directions: Use with the "Puppet Bios" activity on page 71 to create puppet characteristics for future dramatic productions.

Puppet's name:

Puppet's favorite food:

Puppet's favorite thing to do:

Puppet's special talents:

Where your puppet came from:

Members in your puppet's family:

What your puppet is famous for:

Other information:

Performance Critique

Use this page to critique your classmates' performances. Be sure to use kind words.

Name of production: _____

Kind of production (play, Reader's Theater, puppet show): _____

Participant: _____

What did you like about the performance?

_____

_____

What character did you like the most? Why?

_____

_____

What compliments do you have for the actors?

_____

_____

What suggestions do you have for the actors?

_____

_____

Rate the actors in the following areas:

	Excellent	Good	Fair
Voice level:	☐	☐	☐
Rate of speech:	☐	☐	☐
Eye contact:	☐	☐	☐
Expression:	☐	☐	☐

Additional Comments:

_____

_____

References

Aardema, Verna. *Why Mosquitoes Buzz in People's Ears.* Puffin Books, 1978.

Blau, Lisa. *Fall Is Fabulous!: Reader's Theatre Scripts and Extended Activities.* One From the Heart, 1997.

Fredericks, Anthony D. *Frantic Frogs and Other Frankly Fractured Folktales for Readers Theatre.* Teacher Ideas Press, 1993.

Howe, Deborah and James. *Bunnicula.* Avon, 1987.

Kellogg, Steven. *Island of the Skog.* Puffin Books, 1976.

Laughlin, Mildred Knight, and Kathy Howard Latrobe. *Readers Theatre for Children: Scripts and Script Development.* Teacher Ideas Press, 1990.

Laughlin, Mildred Knight, Peggy Tubbs Black, and Margery Kirby Loberg. *Social Studies Readers Theatre for Children: Scripts and Script Development.* Teacher Ideas Press, 1991.

Lobel, Arnold. *Fables.* Demco Media, 1983.

Martin, Justin McCory. *12 Fabulously Funny Fairy Tale Plays.* Instructor Books, 2002.

McBride-Smith, Barbara. *Tell It Together: Foolproof Scripts for Story Theatre.* August House Publishers, 2001.

Shepard, Aaron. *Folktales on Stage: Children's Plays for Reader's Theater, With 16 Play Scripts From World Folk and Fairy Tales and Legends, Including African, Chinese, Southeast Asian, Indian, Middle Eastern, Russian, Scandinavian, and Native American.* Shepard Publications, 2003.

————. *Readers on Stage: Resources for Reader's Theater (or Readers Theatre), with Tips, Play Scripts, and Worksheets.* Shepard Publications, 2004.

————. *Stories on Stage: Scripts for Reader's Theater.* H. W. Wilson, 1993.

Sierra, Judy. *Multicultural Folktales for the Feltboard and Readers' Theater.* Oryx Press, 1996.

Van Laan, Nancy. *Rainbow Crow: A Lenape Tale.* Dragonfly Books, 1991.

White, Melvin R. *Mel White's Readers Theatre Anthology: A Collection of 28 Readings* (Reader's Theater Series), Meriwether Publishing, 1993.

Wolf, Joan, M. and J.M. Wolf. *Cinderella Outgrows the Glass Slipper and Other Zany Fractured Fairy Tale Plays.* Scholastic Professional Books, 2002.